Sweet Halloween: A Fun Coloring Book

Copyright © 2017 SpringMix Media, Inc.

Cover by: Catherine Benante

Illustrations by Catherine Benante and Shutterstock.com

Images are used under license from Shutterstock.com

All rights reserved.

With the exception of photocopying for personal use only, no part of this book may be reproduced in any form by any electronic or mechanical means including photocopying, recording, or information storage and retrieval without permission in writing from the author.

ISBN-13: 978-1546673781

ISBN-10: 1546673784

www.springmixmedia.com

Printed in U.S.A.

Blank page - helps avoid marker bleed-through!

☆ Blank page - helps avoid marker bleed-through!

Blank page - helps avoid marker bleed-through!

☆ Blank page - helps avoid marker bleed-through!

(14) Blank page - helps avoid marker bleed-through!

☆ Blank page - helps avoid marker bleed-through!

(18) Blank page - helps avoid marker bleed-through!

☆ Blank page - helps avoid marker bleed-through!

Blank page - helps avoid marker bleed-through!

☆ Blank page - helps avoid marker bleed-through!

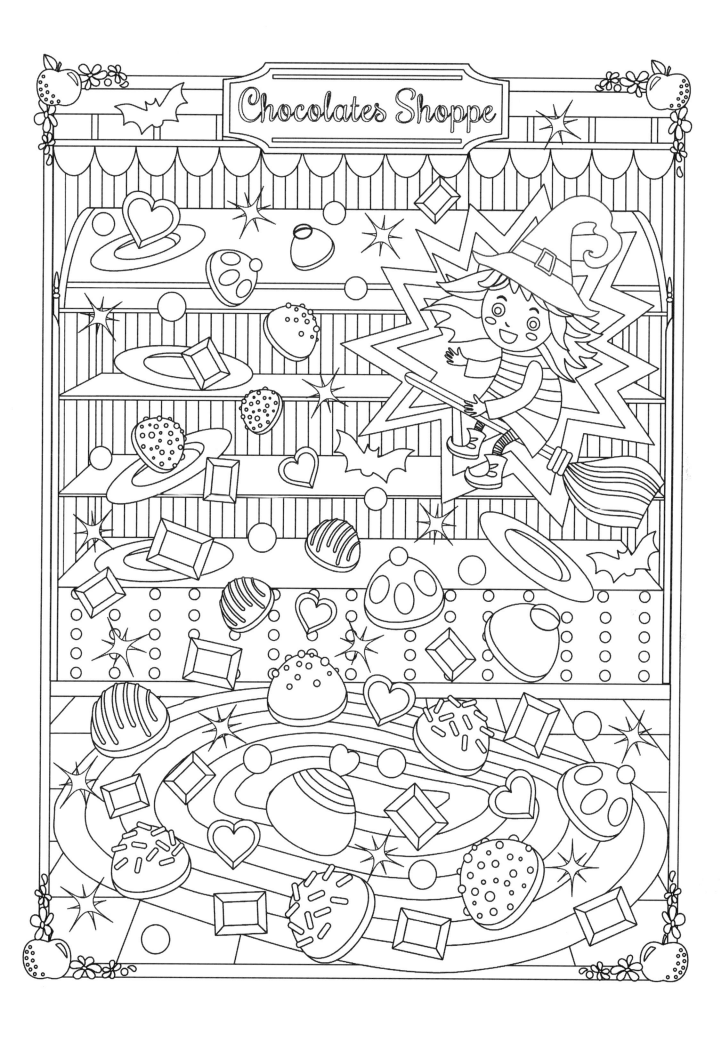

㉖ Blank page - helps avoid marker bleed-through! ☆

☆ Blank page - helps avoid marker bleed-through!

☆ Blank page - helps avoid marker bleed-through!

☆ Blank page - helps avoid marker bleed-through!

38) Blank page - helps avoid marker bleed-through!

☆ Blank page - helps avoid marker bleed-through!

(42) Blank page - helps avoid marker bleed-through! ☆

Blank page - helps avoid marker bleed-through!

☆ Blank page - helps avoid marker bleed-through!

Blank page - helps avoid marker bleed-through!

Blank page - helps avoid marker bleed-through!

Blank page - helps avoid marker bleed-through!

Blank page - helps avoid marker bleed-through!

Blank page - helps avoid marker bleed-through!

☆ Blank page - helps avoid marker bleed-through!

Blank page - helps avoid marker bleed-through!

Blank page - helps avoid marker bleed-through!

Made in the USA
Columbia, SC
03 September 2017